HAL•LEONARD

JAZZ PLAY-ALONG®

Book & Audio for B♭, E♭, C and Bass Clef Instruments

Piazzolla

volume **188**

Arranged and Produced
by Mark Taylor

To access companion recorded performances
and backing tracks, visit:
www.halleonard.com/mylibrary

6191-0077-9214-9554

ISBN 978-1-4950-2032-2

BOOSEY&HAWKES

DISTRIBUTED BY

HAL•LEONARD®

Visit Hal Leonard Online at
www.halleonard.com

World headquarters, contact:
Hal Leonard
7777 West Bluemound Road
Milwaukee, WI 53213
Email: info@halleonard.com

In Europe, contact:
Hal Leonard Europe Limited
42 Wigmore Street
Marylebone, London, W1U 2RN
Email: info@halleonardeurope.com

In Australia, contact:
Hal Leonard Australia Pty. Ltd.
4 Lentara Court
Cheltenham, Victoria, 3192 Australia
Email: info@halleonard.com.au

BOOK

TITLE	PAGE NUMBERS			
	C Treble Instruments	B♭ Instruments	E♭ Instruments	C Bass Instruments
Ausencias (The Absent)	4	24	44	64
El viaje (The Voyage)	6	26	46	66
La chanson du Popo (The Song of Popo)	8	28	48	68
Libertango	9	29	49	69
Milonga	10	30	50	70
Oblivion	12	32	52	72
Sensuel (Sensual)	17	37	57	77
Sin rumbo (Aimless)	21	41	61	81
Street Tango	14	34	54	74
Vuelvo al sur (I'm Returning South)	20	40	60	80

AUDIO

TITLE	Audio Track Number Split Track/Melody	Audio Track Number Full Stereo Track
Ausencias (The Absent)	1	2
El viaje (The Voyage)	3	4
La chanson du Popo (The Song of Popo)	5	6
Libertango	7	8
Milonga	9	10
Oblivion	11	12
Sensuel (Sensual)	13	14
Sin rumbo (Aimless)	15	16
Street Tango	17	18
Vuelvo al sur (I'm Returning South)	19	20
B♭ Tuning Notes		21

PIAZZOLLA

Volume 188

Arranged and Produced
by Mark Taylor

Featured Players:

Graham Breedlove–Trumpet
John Desalme–Saxes
Tony Nalker–Piano
Jim Roberts–Guitar
Paul Henry–Bass
Todd Harrison–Drums
Joan Grauman–Accordion

Recorded at Bias Studios, Springfield, Virginia
Bob Dawson, Engineer

HOW TO USE THE AUDIO:

Each song has <u>two</u> tracks:

1) Split Track/Melody

Woodwind, Brass, Keyboard, and **Mallet Players** can use this track as a learning tool for melody style and inflection.

Bass Players can learn and perform with this track – remove the recorded bass track by turning down the volume on the LEFT channel.

Keyboard and **Guitar Players** can learn and perform with this track – remove the recorded piano part by turning down the volume on the RIGHT channel.

2) Full Stereo Track

Soloists or **Groups** can learn and perform with this accompaniment track with the RHYTHM SECTION only.

AUDIO
1 : SPLIT TRACK/MELODY
2 : FULL STEREO TRACK

C VERSION

AUSENCIAS
(THE ABSENT)

BY ASTOR PIAZZOLLA

AUDIO
3 : SPLIT TRACK/MELODY
4 : FULL STEREO TRACK

C VERSION

EL VIAJE
(THE VOYAGE)

BY ASTOR PIAZZOLLA

AUDIO

5 : SPLIT TRACK/MELODY
6 : FULL STEREO TRACK

C VERSION

LA CHANSON DU POPO
(THE SONG OF POPO)

FROM FAMILLE D'ARTISTES

BY ASTOR PIAZZOLLA

LIBERTANGO

BY ASTOR PIAZZOLLA

C VERSION

AUDIO
◆ 9 : SPLIT TRACK/MELODY
◆ 10 : FULL STEREO TRACK

C VERSION

MILONGA
FROM A MIDSUMMER NIGHT'S DREAM

BY ASTOR PIAZZOLLA

AUDIO

◆11◆ : SPLIT TRACK/MELODY
◆12◆ : FULL STEREO TRACK

C VERSION

OBLIVION

BY ASTOR PIAZZOLLA

STREET TANGO

BY ASTOR PIAZZOLLA

AUDIO
17 : SPLIT TRACK/MELODY
18 : FULL STEREO TRACK

C VERSION

SENSUEL
(SENSUAL)
FROM A MIDSUMMER NIGHT'S DREAM

C VERSION

BY ASTOR PIAZZOLLA

VUELVO AL SUR
(I'M RETURNING SOUTH)

BY ASTOR PIAZZOLLA

AUDIO
19: SPLIT TRACK/MELODY
20: FULL STEREO TRACK

C VERSION

AUDIO
15: SPLIT TRACK/MELODY
16: FULL STEREO TRACK

C VERSION

SIN RUMBO
(AIMLESS)

BY ASTOR PIAZZOLLA

AUDIO
1 : SPLIT TRACK/MELODY
2 : FULL STEREO TRACK

Bb VERSION

AUSENCIAS
(THE ABSENT)

BY ASTOR PIAZZOLLA

AUDIO

3 : SPLIT TRACK/MELODY
4 : FULL STEREO TRACK

Bb VERSION

EL VIAJE
(THE VOYAGE)

BY ASTOR PIAZZOLLA

LA CHANSON DU POPO
(THE SONG OF POPO)

FROM FAMILLE D'ARTISTES

BY ASTOR PIAZZOLLA

Bb VERSION

LIBERTANGO

BY ASTOR PIAZZOLLA

AUDIO
◆9◆: SPLIT TRACK/MELODY
◆10◆: FULL STEREO TRACK

MILONGA
FROM A MIDSUMMER NIGHT'S DREAM

BY ASTOR PIAZZOLLA

Bb VERSION

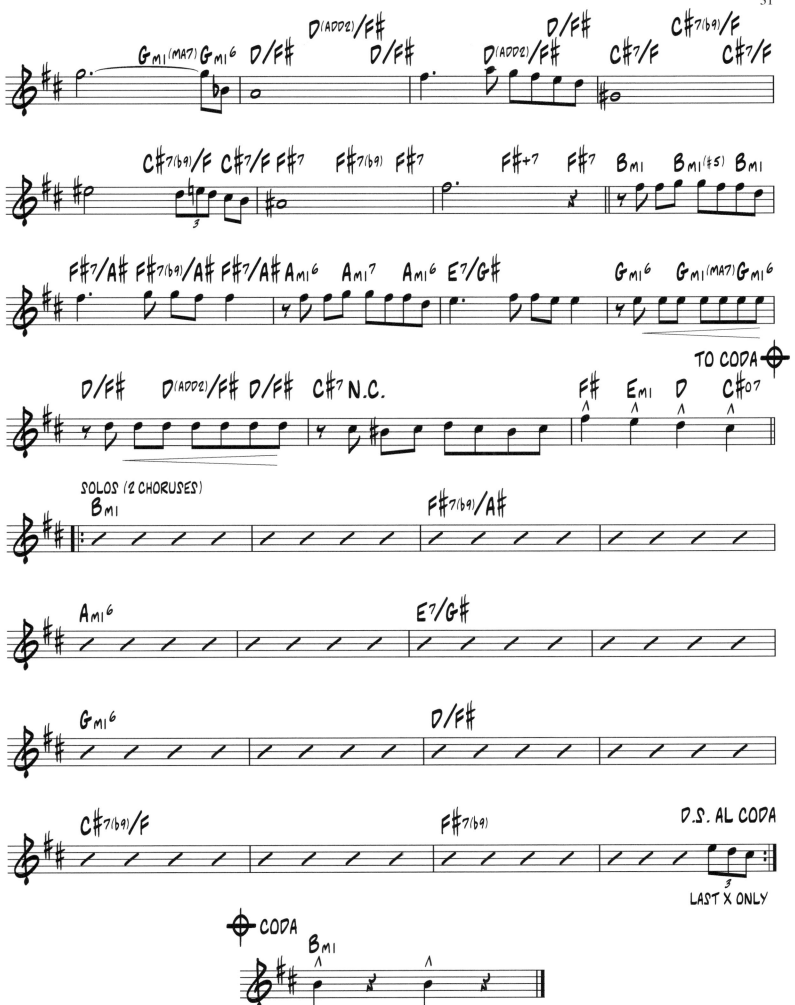

AUDIO
11 : SPLIT TRACK/MELODY
12 : FULL STEREO TRACK

OBLIVION

BY ASTOR PIAZZOLLA

Bb VERSION

STREET TANGO

BY ASTOR PIAZZOLLA

AUDIO
- **17** : SPLIT TRACK/MELODY
- **18** : FULL STEREO TRACK

Bb VERSION

AUDIO
13 : SPLIT TRACK/MELODY
14 : FULL STEREO TRACK

SENSUEL
(SENSUAL)
FROM A MIDSUMMER NIGHT'S DREAM

Bb VERSION

BY ASTOR PIAZZOLLA

VUELVO AL SUR
(I'M RETURNING SOUTH)

BY ASTOR PIAZZOLLA

SIN RUMBO
(AIMLESS)

BY ASTOR PIAZZOLLA

AUDIO
- 15 : SPLIT TRACK/MELODY
- 16 : FULL STEREO TRACK

Bb VERSION

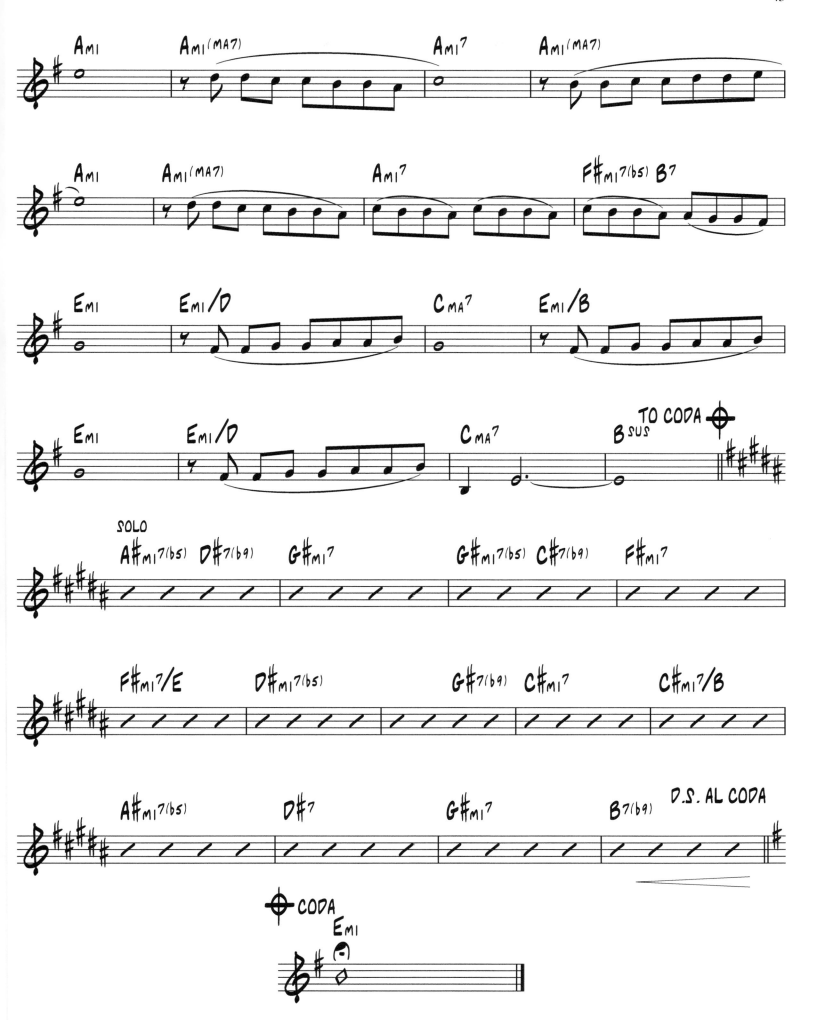

AUSENCIAS
(THE ABSENT)

BY ASTOR PIAZZOLLA

RIT.   A TEMPO

AUDIO
❸ : SPLIT TRACK/MELODY
❹ : FULL STEREO TRACK

Eb VERSION

EL VIAJE
(THE VOYAGE)

BY ASTOR PIAZZOLLA

AUDIO
5 : SPLIT TRACK/MELODY
6 : FULL STEREO TRACK

Eb VERSION

LA CHANSON DU POPO
(THE SONG OF POPO)
FROM FAMILLE D'ARTISTES

BY ASTOR PIAZZOLLA

LIBERTANGO

BY ASTOR PIAZZOLLA

AUDIO
◆7: SPLIT TRACK/MELODY
◆8: FULL STEREO TRACK

Eb VERSION

AUDIO
9 : SPLIT TRACK/MELODY
10 : FULL STEREO TRACK

Eb VERSION

MILONGA
FROM A MIDSUMMER NIGHT'S DREAM

BY ASTOR PIAZZOLLA

OBLIVION

Eb VERSION

BY ASTOR PIAZZOLLA

STREET TANGO

BY ASTOR PIAZZOLLA

AUDIO
13 : SPLIT TRACK/MELODY
14 : FULL STEREO TRACK

SENSUEL
(SENSUAL)
FROM A MIDSUMMER NIGHT'S DREAM

Eb VERSION

BY ASTOR PIAZZOLLA

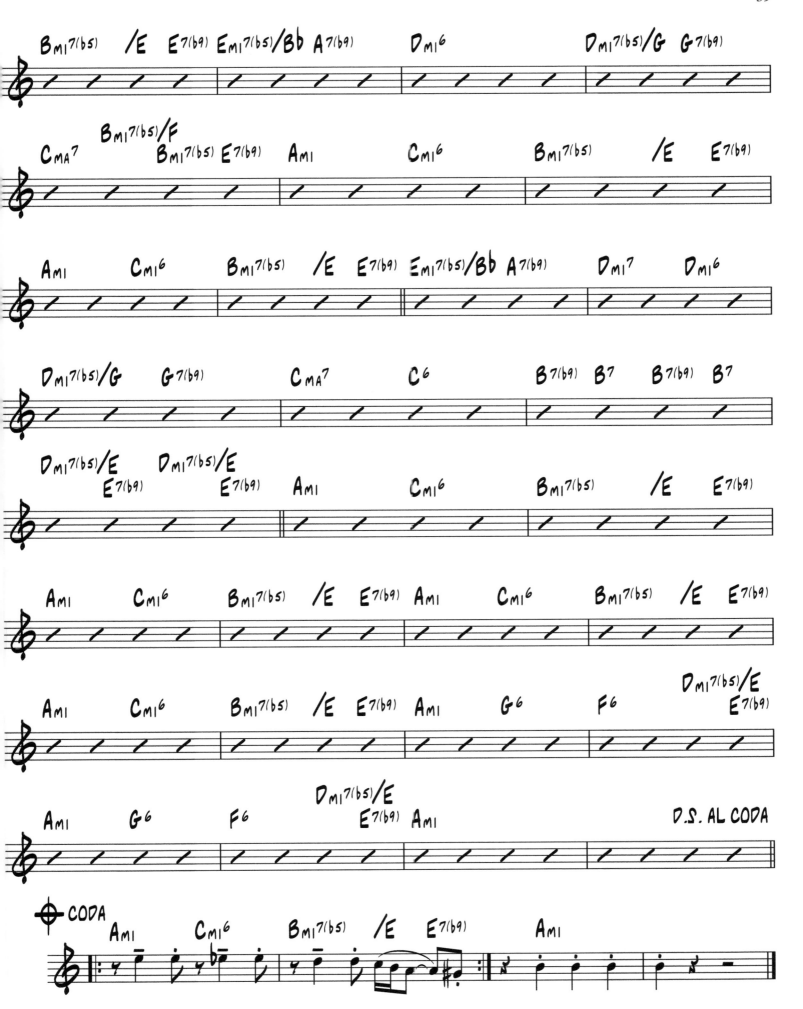

SIN RUMBO
(AIMLESS)

BY ASTOR PIAZZOLLA

AUDIO
15 : SPLIT TRACK/MELODY
16 : FULL STEREO TRACK

Eb VERSION

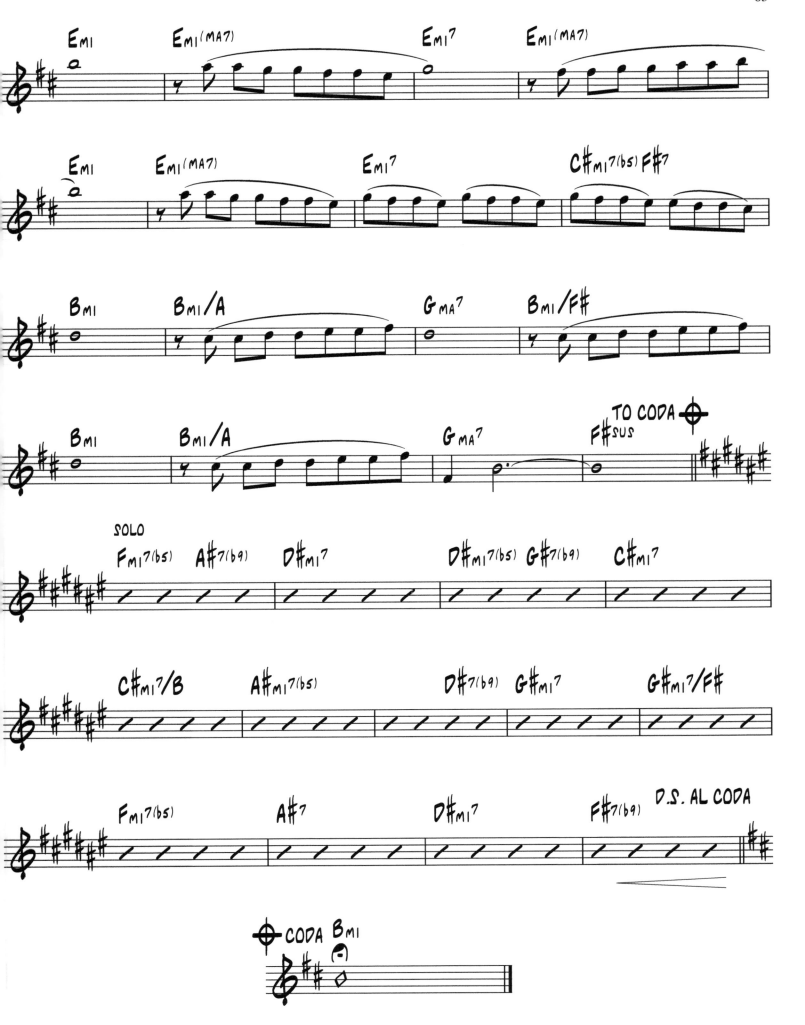

AUSENCIAS
(THE ABSENT)

BY ASTOR PIAZZOLLA

EL VIAJE
(THE VOYAGE)

BY ASTOR PIAZZOLLA

67

AUDIO

5 : SPLIT TRACK/MELODY
6 : FULL STEREO TRACK

𝄢 : C VERSION

LA CHANSON DU POPO
(THE SONG OF POPO)
FROM FAMILLE D'ARTISTES

BY ASTOR PIAZZOLLA

LIBERTANGO

BY ASTOR PIAZZOLLA

AUDIO
⟨9⟩ : SPLIT TRACK/MELODY
⟨10⟩ : FULL STEREO TRACK

MILONGA
FROM A MIDSUMMER NIGHT'S DREAM

BY ASTOR PIAZZOLLA

𝄢: C VERSION

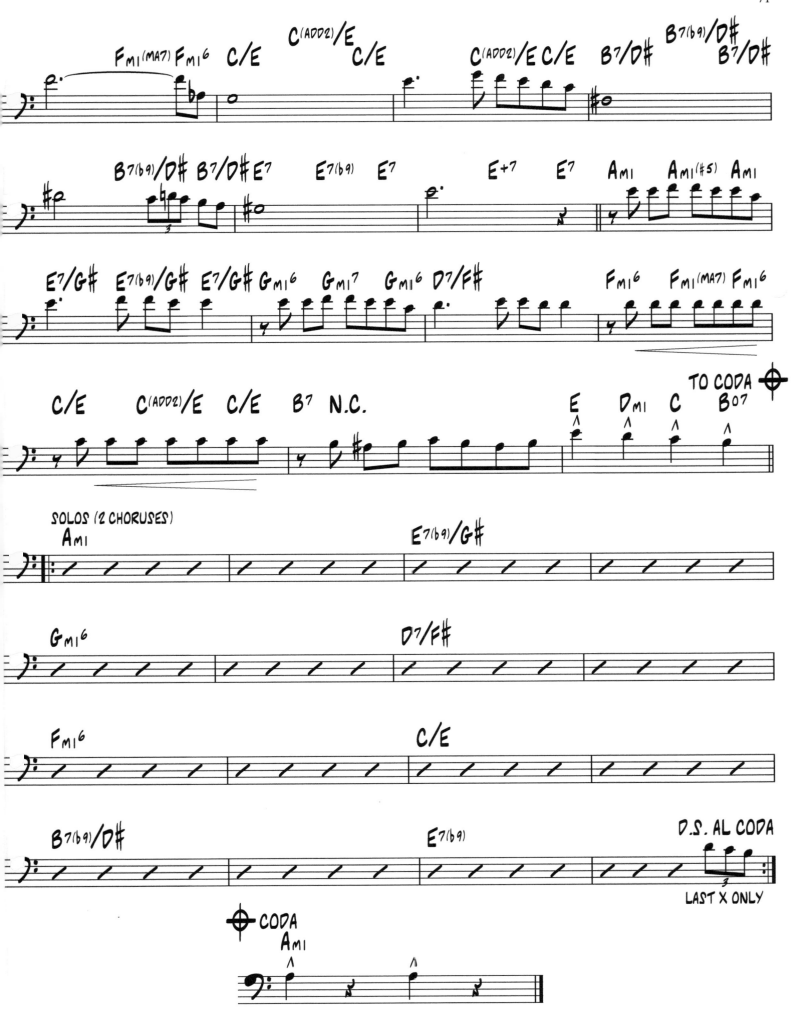

OBLIVION

BY ASTOR PIAZZOLLA

C VERSION

STREET TANGO

BY ASTOR PIAZZOLLA

AUDIO
17 : SPLIT TRACK/MELODY
18 : FULL STEREO TRACK

C VERSION

AUDIO
13: SPLIT TRACK/MELODY
14: FULL STEREO TRACK

🎼: C VERSION

SENSUEL
(SENSUAL)
FROM A MIDSUMMER NIGHT'S DREAM

BY ASTOR PIAZZOLLA

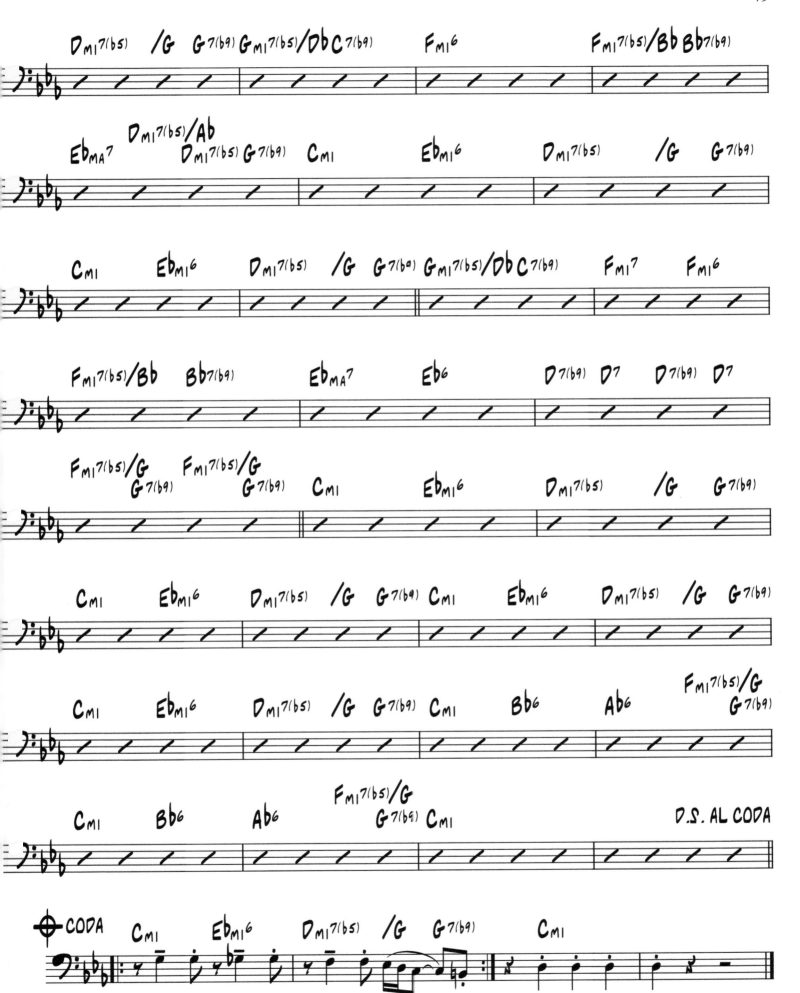

SIN RUMBO
(AIMLESS)

BY ASTOR PIAZZOLLA

C VERSION

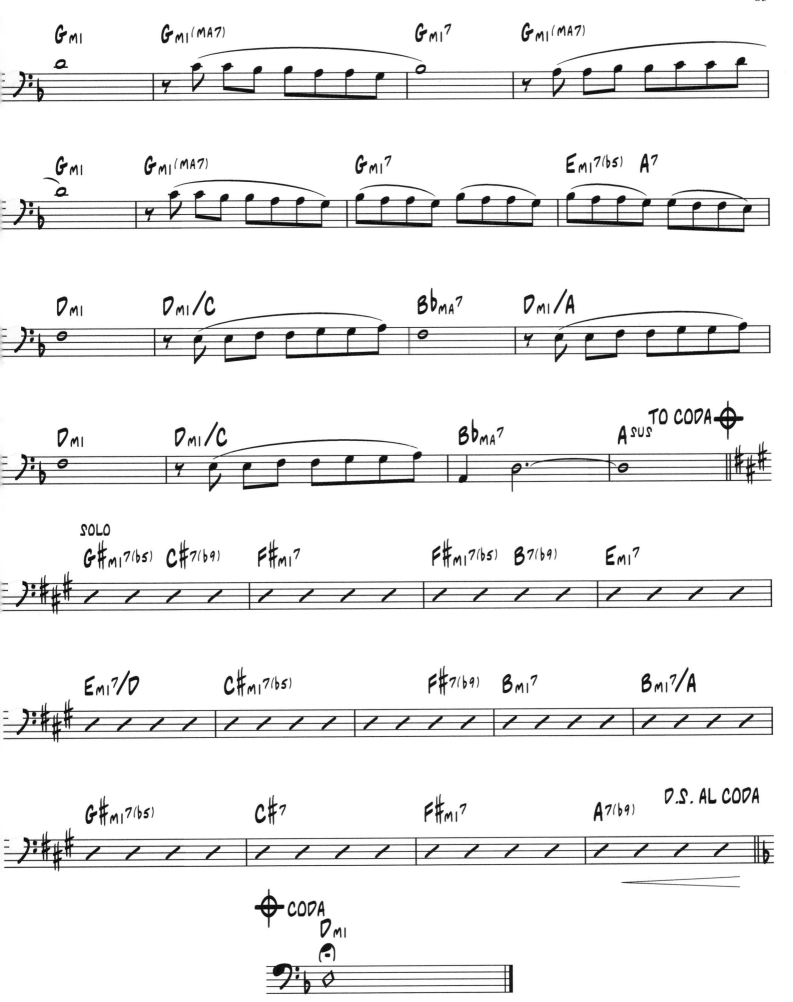

Presenting the Hal Leonard JAZZ PLAY-ALONG® SERIES

For use with all B-flat, E-flat, Bass Clef and C instruments, the Jazz Play-Along® Series is the ultimate learning tool for all jazz musicians. With musician-friendly lead sheets, melody cues, and other split-track audio choices included, these first-of-a-kind packages help you master improvisation while playing some of the greatest tunes of all time. FOR STUDY, each tune includes a split track with: melody cue with proper style and inflection • professional rhythm tracks • choruses for soloing • removable bass part • removable piano part. FOR PERFORMANCE, each tune also has: an additional full stereo accompaniment track (no melody) • additional choruses for soloing.

1A. MAIDEN VOYAGE/ALL BLUES
00843158 ...... $22.99

1. DUKE ELLINGTON
00841644...... $16.99

2. MILES DAVIS
00841645...... $17.99

3. THE BLUES
00841646...... $19.99

4. JAZZ BALLADS
00841691...... $17.99

5. BEST OF BEBOP
00841689...... $17.99

6. JAZZ CLASSICS WITH EASY CHANGES
00841690...... $16.99

7. ESSENTIAL JAZZ STANDARDS
00843000...... $17.99

8. ANTONIO CARLOS JOBIM AND THE ART OF THE BOSSA NOVA
00843001...... $16.99

9. DIZZY GILLESPIE
00843002...... $19.99

10. DISNEY CLASSICS
00843003...... $16.99

12. ESSENTIAL JAZZ CLASSICS
00843005...... $16.99

13. JOHN COLTRANE
00843006...... $17.99

14. IRVING BERLIN
00843007...... $16.99

15. RODGERS & HAMMERSTEIN
00843008...... $16.99

16. COLE PORTER
00843009...... $17.99

17. COUNT BASIE
00843010...... $17.99

18. HAROLD ARLEN
00843011...... $17.99

20. CHRISTMAS CAROLS
00843080...... $16.99

21. RODGERS AND HART CLASSICS
00843014...... $16.99

22. WAYNE SHORTER
00843015...... $17.99

23. LATIN JAZZ
00843016...... $19.99

24. EARLY JAZZ STANDARDS
00843017...... $16.99

25. CHRISTMAS JAZZ
00843018...... $17.99

26. CHARLIE PARKER
00843019...... $16.99

27. GREAT JAZZ STANDARDS
00843020...... $17.99

28. BIG BAND ERA
00843021...... $17.99

29. LENNON AND MCCARTNEY
00843022...... $24.99

30. BLUES' BEST
00843023...... $16.99

31. JAZZ IN THREE
00843024...... $16.99

32. BEST OF SWING
00843025...... $17.99

33. SONNY ROLLINS
00843029...... $16.99

34. ALL TIME STANDARDS
00843030...... $17.99

35. BLUESY JAZZ
00843031...... $17.99

36. HORACE SILVER
00843032...... $19.99

37. BILL EVANS
00843033...... $16.99

38. YULETIDE JAZZ
00843034...... $16.99

39. "ALL THE THINGS YOU ARE" & MORE JEROME KERN SONGS
00843035...... $19.99

40. BOSSA NOVA
00843036...... $19.99

41. CLASSIC DUKE ELLINGTON
00843037...... $16.99

42. GERRY MULLIGAN FAVORITES
00843038...... $16.99

43. GERRY MULLIGAN CLASSICS
00843039...... $19.99

45. GEORGE GERSHWIN
00103643...... $24.99

47. CLASSIC JAZZ BALLADS
00843043...... $17.99

48. BEBOP CLASSICS
00843044...... $16.99

49. MILES DAVIS STANDARDS
00843045...... $19.99

52. STEVIE WONDER
00843048...... $17.99

53. RHYTHM CHANGES
00843049...... $16.99

55. BENNY GOLSON
00843052...... $19.99

56. "GEORGIA ON MY MIND" & OTHER SONGS BY HOAGY CARMICHAEL
00843056...... $17.99

57. VINCE GUARALDI
00843057...... $16.99

58. MORE LENNON AND MCCARTNEY
00843059...... $17.99

59. SOUL JAZZ
00843060...... $17.99

60. DEXTER GORDON
00843061...... $16.99

61. MONGO SANTAMARIA
00843062...... $16.99

62. JAZZ-ROCK FUSION
00843063...... $19.99

63. CLASSICAL JAZZ
00843064...... $16.99

64. TV TUNES
00843065...... $16.99

65. SMOOTH JAZZ
00843066...... $19.99

66. A CHARLIE BROWN CHRISTMAS
00843067...... $16.99

67. CHICK COREA
00843068...... $22.99

68. CHARLES MINGUS
00843069...... $19.99

71. COLE PORTER CLASSICS
00843073...... $16.99

72. CLASSIC JAZZ BALLADS
00843074...... $16.99

73. JAZZ/BLUES
00843075...... $16.99

74. BEST JAZZ CLASSICS
00843076...... $16.99

75. PAUL DESMOND
00843077...... $17.99

78. STEELY DAN
00843070...... $19.99

79. MILES DAVIS CLASSICS
00843081...... $16.99

80. JIMI HENDRIX
00843083...... $17.99

83. ANDREW LLOYD WEBBER
00843104...... $16.99

84. BOSSA NOVA CLASSICS
00843105...... $17.99

85. MOTOWN HITS
00843109...... $17.99

86. BENNY GOODMAN
00843110...... $17.99

87. DIXIELAND
00843111...... $16.99

90. THELONIOUS MONK CLASSICS
00841262 ....$16.99

91. THELONIOUS MONK FAVORITES
00841263 ....$17.99

92. LEONARD BERNSTEIN
00450134 ....$16.99

93. DISNEY FAVORITES
00843142 ....$16.99

94. RAY
00843143 ....$19.99

95. JAZZ AT THE LOUNGE
00843144 ....$17.99

96. LATIN JAZZ STANDARDS
00843145 ....$16.99

97. MAYBE I'M AMAZED*
00843148 ....$16.99

98. DAVE FRISHBERG
00843149 ....$16.99

99. SWINGING STANDARDS
00843150 ....$16.99

100. LOUIS ARMSTRONG
00740423 ....$19.99

101. BUD POWELL
00843152 ....$16.99

102. JAZZ POP
00843153 ....$19.99

**103. ON GREEN DOLPHIN STREET
& OTHER JAZZ CLASSICS**
00843154 ....$16.99

104. ELTON JOHN
00843155 ....$19.99

105. SOULFUL JAZZ
00843151 ....$17.99

106. SLO' JAZZ
00843117 ....$16.99

107. MOTOWN CLASSICS
00843116 ....$17.99

108. JAZZ WALTZ
00843159 ....$16.99

109. OSCAR PETERSON
00843160 ....$16.99

110. JUST STANDARDS
00843161 ....$16.99

111. COOL CHRISTMAS
00843162 ....$16.99

112. PAQUITO D'RIVERA – LATIN JAZZ*
48020662 ....$16.99

113. PAQUITO D'RIVERA – BRAZILIAN JAZZ*
48020663 ....$19.99

114. MODERN JAZZ QUARTET FAVORITES
00843163 ....$16.99

115. THE SOUND OF MUSIC
00843164 ....$16.99

116. JACO PASTORIUS
00843165 ....$17.99

117. ANTONIO CARLOS JOBIM – MORE HITS
00843166 ....$17.99

118. BIG JAZZ STANDARDS COLLECTION
00843167 ....$27.50

119. JELLY ROLL MORTON
00843168 ....$16.99

120. J.S. BACH
00843169 ....$17.99

121. DJANGO REINHARDT
00843170 ....$16.99

122. PAUL SIMON
00843182 ....$16.99

123. BACHARACH & DAVID
00843185 ....$16.99

124. JAZZ-ROCK HORN HITS
00843186 ....$16.99

125. SAMMY NESTICO
00843187 ....$16.99

126. COUNT BASIE CLASSICS
00843157 ....$16.99

127. CHUCK MANGIONE
00843188 ....$19.99

128. VOCAL STANDARDS (LOW VOICE)
00843189 ....$16.99

129. VOCAL STANDARDS (HIGH VOICE)
00843190 ....$16.99

130. VOCAL JAZZ (LOW VOICE)
00843191 ....$16.99

131. VOCAL JAZZ (HIGH VOICE)
00843192 ....$16.99

132. STAN GETZ ESSENTIALS
00843193 ....$17.99

133. STAN GETZ FAVORITES
00843194 ....$16.99

134. NURSERY RHYMES*
00843196 ....$17.99

135. JEFF BECK
00843197 ....$16.99

136. NAT ADDERLEY
00843198 ....$16.99

137. WES MONTGOMERY
00843199 ....$16.99

138. FREDDIE HUBBARD
00843200 ....$16.99

139. JULIAN "CANNONBALL" ADDERLEY
00843201 ....$16.99

140. JOE ZAWINUL
00843202 ....$16.99

141. BILL EVANS STANDARDS
00843156 ....$16.99

142. CHARLIE PARKER GEMS
00843222 ....$16.99

143. JUST THE BLUES
00843223 ....$16.99

144. LEE MORGAN
00843229 ....$16.99

145. COUNTRY STANDARDS
00843230 ....$16.99

146. RAMSEY LEWIS
00843231 ....$16.99

147. SAMBA
00843232 ....$16.99

148. JOHN COLTRANE FAVORITES
00843233 ....$16.99

149. JOHN COLTRANE – GIANT STEPS
00843234 ....$16.99

150. JAZZ IMPROV BASICS
00843195 ....$19.99

151. MODERN JAZZ QUARTET CLASSICS
00843209 ....$16.99

152. J.J. JOHNSON
00843210 ....$16.99

153. KENNY GARRETT
00843212 ....$16.99

154. HENRY MANCINI
00843213 ....$17.99

155. SMOOTH JAZZ CLASSICS
00843215 ....$17.99

156. THELONIOUS MONK – EARLY GEMS
00843216 ....$16.99

157. HYMNS
00843217 ....$16.99

158. JAZZ COVERS ROCK
00843219 ....$16.99

159. MOZART
00843220 ....$16.99

160. GEORGE SHEARING
14041531 ....$16.99

161. DAVE BRUBECK
14041556 ....$16.99

162. BIG CHRISTMAS COLLECTION
00843221 ....$24.99

163. JOHN COLTRANE STANDARDS
00843235 ....$16.99

164. HERB ALPERT
14041775 ....$19.99

165. GEORGE BENSON
00843240 ....$17.99

166. ORNETTE COLEMAN
00843241 ....$16.99

167. JOHNNY MANDEL
00103642 ....$16.99

168. TADD DAMERON
00103663 ....$16.99

169. BEST JAZZ STANDARDS
00109249 ....$24.99

170. ULTIMATE JAZZ STANDARDS
00109250 ....$24.99

171. RADIOHEAD
00109305 ....$16.99

172. POP STANDARDS
00111669 ....$16.99

174. TIN PAN ALLEY
00119125 ....$16.99

175. TANGO
00119836 ....$16.99

176. JOHNNY MERCER
00119838 ....$16.99

177. THE II-V-I PROGRESSION
00843239 ....$24.99

178. JAZZ/FUNK
00121902 ....$17.99

179. MODAL JAZZ
00122273 ....$16.99

180. MICHAEL JACKSON
00122327 ....$17.99

181. BILLY JOEL
00122329 ....$19.99

**182. "RHAPSODY IN BLUE" & 7 OTHER
CLASSICAL-BASED JAZZ PIECES**
00116847 ....$16.99

183. SONDHEIM
00126253 ....$16.99

184. JIMMY SMITH
00126943 ....$17.99

185. JAZZ FUSION
00127558 ....$17.99

186. JOE PASS
00128391 ....$16.99

187. CHRISTMAS FAVORITES
00128393 ....$16.99

188. PIAZZOLLA – 10 FAVORITE TUNES
48023253 ....$16.99

189. JOHN LENNON
00138678 ....$16.99

*These do not include split tracks.

JAZZ INSTRUCTION & IMPROVISATION

500 JAZZ LICKS
by Brent Vaartstra

This book aims to assist you on your journey to play jazz fluently. These short phrases and ideas we call "licks" will help you understand how to navigate the common chords and chord progressions you will encounter. Adding this vocabulary to your arsenal will send you down the right path and improve your jazz playing, regardless of your instrument.
00142384 ....$16.99

1001 JAZZ LICKS
by Jack Shneidman
Cherry Lane Music

This book presents 1,001 melodic gems played over dozens of the most important chord progressions heard in jazz. This is the ideal book for beginners seeking a well-organized, easy-to-follow encyclopedia of jazz vocabulary, as well as professionals who want to take their knowledge of the jazz language to new heights.
02500133 ....$17.99

THE BERKLEE BOOK OF JAZZ HARMONY
by Joe Mulholland & Tom Hojnacki

Learn jazz harmony, as taught at Berklee College of Music. This text provides a strong foundation in harmonic principles, supporting further study in jazz composition, arranging, and improvisation. It covers basic chord types and their tensions, with practical demonstrations of how they are used in characteristic jazz contexts and an accompanying recording that lets you hear how they can be applied.
00113755 Book/Online Audio....................................$29.99

BUILDING A JAZZ VOCABULARY
By Mike Steinel

A valuable resource for learning the basics of jazz from Mike Steinel of the University of North Texas. It covers: the basics of jazz • how to build effective solos • a comprehensive practice routine • and a jazz vocabulary of the masters.
00849911 ....$19.99

COMPREHENSIVE TECHNIQUE FOR JAZZ MUSICIANS
2ND EDITION
by Bert Ligon
Houston Publishing

An incredible presentation of the most practical exercises an aspiring jazz student could want. All are logically interwoven with fine "real world" examples from jazz to classical. This book is an essential anthology of technical, compositional, and theoretical exercises, with lots of musical examples.
00030455 ....$34.99

EAR TRAINING
by Keith Wyatt,
Carl Schroeder and Joe Elliott
Musicians Institute Press

Covers: basic pitch matching • singing major and minor scales • identifying intervals • transcribing melodies and rhythm • identifying chords and progressions • seventh chords and the blues • modal interchange, chromaticism, modulation • and more.
00695198 Book/Online Audio....................................$29.99

EXERCISES AND ETUDES FOR THE JAZZ INSTRUMENTALIST
by J.J. Johnson

Designed as study material and playable by any instrument, these pieces run the gamut of the jazz experience, featuring common and uncommon time signatures and keys, and styles from ballads to funk. They are progressively graded so that both beginners and professionals will be challenged by the demands of this wonderful music.
00842018 Bass Clef Edition $19.99
00842042 Treble Clef Edition $16.95

HOW TO PLAY FROM A REAL BOOK
by Robert Rawlins

Explore, understand, and perform the songs in real books with the techniques in this book. Learn how to analyze the form and harmonic structure, insert an introduction, interpret the melody, improvise on the chords, construct bass lines, voice the chords, add substitutions, and more. It addresses many aspects of solo and small band performance that can improve your own playing and your understanding of what others are doing around you.
00312097 ....$19.99

JAZZ DUETS
ETUDES FOR PHRASING
AND ARTICULATION
by Richard Lowell
Berklee Press

With these 27 duets in jazz and jazz-influenced styles, you will learn how to improve your ear, sense of timing, phrasing, and your facility in bringing theoretical principles into musical expression. Covers: jazz staccato & legato • scales, modes & harmonies • phrasing within and between measures • swing feel • and more.
00302151 ....$14.99

JAZZ THEORY & WORKBOOK
by Lilian Dericq &
Étienne Guéreau

Designed for all instrumentalists, this book teaches how jazz standards are constructed. It is also a great resource for arrangers and composers seeking new writing tools. While some of the musical examples are pianistic, this book is not exclusively for keyboard players.
00159022 ....$19.99

JAZZ THEORY RESOURCES
by Bert Ligon
Houston Publishing, Inc.

This is a jazz theory text in two volumes. **Volume 1 includes**: review of basic theory • rhythm in jazz performance • triadic generalization • diatonic harmonic progressions and analysis • substitutions and turnarounds • and more. **Volume 2 includes**: modes and modal frameworks • quartal harmony • extended tertian structures and triadic superimposition • pentatonic applications • coloring "outside" the lines and beyond • and more.
00030458 Volume 1 ....$39.99
00030459 Volume 2 ....$32.99

JAZZOLOGY
THE ENCYCLOPEDIA OF JAZZ THEORY FOR ALL MUSICIANS
by Robert Rawlins and
Nor Eddine Bahha

This comprehensive resource covers a variety of jazz topics, for beginners and pros of any instrument. The book serves as an encyclopedia for reference, a thorough methodology for the student, and a workbook for the classroom.
00311167 ....$24.99

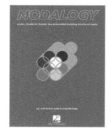

MODALOGY
SCALES, MODES & CHORDS: THE PRIMORDIAL BUILDING BLOCKS OF MUSIC
by Jeff Brent with Schell Barkley

Primarily a music theory reference, this book presents a unique perspective on the origins, interlocking aspects, and usage of the most common scales and modes in occidental music. Anyone wishing to seriously explore the realms of scales, modes, and their real-world functions will find the most important issues dealt with in meticulous detail within these pages.
00312274 ....$24.99

THE SOURCE
THE DICTIONARY OF CONTEMPORARY AND TRADITIONAL SCALES
by Steve Barta

This book serves as an informative guide for people who are looking for good, solid information regarding scales, chords, and how they work together. It provides right and left hand fingerings for scales, chords, and complete inversions. Includes over 20 different scales, each written in all 12 keys.
00240885 ....$19.99

HAL•LEONARD®
www.halleonard.com

Prices, contents & availability
subject to change without notice.

ARTIST TRANSCRIPTIONS

Artist Transcriptions are authentic, note-for-note transcriptions of today's hottest artists in jazz, pop and rock. These outstanding, accurate arrangements are in an easy-to-read format which includes all essential lines. **Artist Transcriptions** can be used to perform, sequence or for reference.

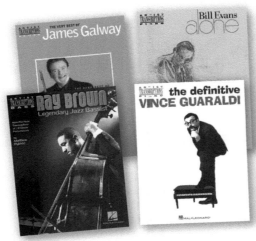

CLARINET

00672423	Buddy De Franco Collection	$19.95

FLUTE

00672379	Eric Dolphy Collection	$19.95
00672582	The Very Best of James Galway	$19.99
00672372	James Moody Collection – Sax and Flute	$19.95

GUITAR & BASS

00660113	Guitar Style of George Benson	$19.99
00672573	Ray Brown – Legendary Jazz Bassist	$22.99
00672331	Ron Carter Collection	$19.99
00660115	Al Di Meola – Friday Night in San Francisco	$17.99
00604043	Al Di Meola – Music, Words, Pictures	$14.95
00125617	Best of Herb Ellis	$19.99
00673245	Jazz Style of Tal Farlow	$24.99
00699306	Jim Hall – Exploring Jazz Guitar	$19.99
00672353	The Joe Pass Collection	$19.99
00673216	John Patitucci	$17.99
00672374	Johnny Smith – Guitar Solos	$24.99
00672320	Mark Whitfield Guitar Collection	$19.95

PIANO & KEYBOARD

00672338	The Monty Alexander Collection	$19.95
00672487	Monty Alexander Plays Standards	$19.95
00672520	Count Basie Collection	$19.95
00192307	Bebop Piano Legends	$19.99
00113680	Blues Piano Legends	$22.99
00672526	The Bill Charlap Collection	$19.99
00278003	A Charlie Brown Christmas	$17.99
00672439	Cyrus Chestnut Collection	$19.95
00672300	Chick Corea – Paint the World	$19.99
00146105	Bill Evans – Alone	$19.99
00672548	The Mastery of Bill Evans	$16.99
00672425	Bill Evans – Piano Interpretations	$22.99
00672365	Bill Evans – Play Standards	$22.99
00121885	Bill Evans – Time Remembered	$19.99
00672510	Bill Evans Trio Vol. 1: 1959-1961	$27.99
00672511	Bill Evans Trio Vol. 2: 1962-1965	$27.99
00672512	Bill Evans Trio Vol. 3: 1968-1974	$29.99
00672513	Bill Evans Trio Vol. 4: 1979-1980	$24.95
00193332	Erroll Garner – Concert by the Sea	$22.99
00672486	Vince Guaraldi Collection	$19.99
00289644	The Definitive Vince Guaraldi	$34.99
00672419	Herbie Hancock Collection	$22.99
00672438	Hampton Hawes Collection	$19.95

00672322	Ahmad Jamal Collection	$24.99
00255671	Jazz Piano Masterpieces	$19.99
00124367	Jazz Piano Masters Play Rodgers & Hammerstein	$19.99
00672564	Best of Jeff Lorber	$19.99
00672476	Brad Mehldau Collection	$22.99
00672388	Best of Thelonious Monk	$22.99
00672389	Thelonious Monk Collection	$24.99
00672390	Thelonious Monk Plays Jazz Standards – Volume 1	$22.99
00672391	Thelonious Monk Plays Jazz Standards – Volume 2	$22.99
00672433	Jelly Roll Morton – The Piano Rolls	$17.99
00672553	Charlie Parker Piano featuring The Paul Smith Trio (Book/CD)	$19.95
00264094	Oscar Peterson – Night Train	$19.99
00672544	Oscar Peterson – Originals	$14.99
00672531	Oscar Peterson – Plays Duke Ellington	$24.99
00672563	Oscar Peterson – A Royal Wedding Suite	$19.99
00672569	Oscar Peterson – Tracks	$19.99
00672533	Oscar Peterson – Trios	$29.99
00672534	Very Best of Oscar Peterson	$22.95
00672371	Bud Powell Classics	$22.99
00672376	Bud Powell Collection	$24.99
00672507	Gonzalo Rubalcaba Collection	$19.95
00672303	Horace Silver Collection	$24.99
00672316	Art Tatum Collection	$24.99
00672355	Art Tatum Solo Book	$19.99
00672357	The Billy Taylor Collection	$24.95
00673215	McCoy Tyner	$22.99
00672321	Cedar Walton Collection	$19.95
00672519	Kenny Werner Collection	$19.95
00672434	Teddy Wilson Collection	$22.99

SAXOPHONE

00672566	The Mindi Abair Collection	$14.99
00673244	Julian "Cannonball" Adderley Collection	$22.99
00673237	Michael Brecker	$19.99
00672429	Michael Brecker Collection	$24.99
00672394	James Carter Collection	$19.95
00672529	John Coltrane – Giant Steps	$17.99
00672494	John Coltrane – A Love Supreme	$16.99
00672493	John Coltrane Plays "Coltrane Changes"	$19.95
00672453	John Coltrane Plays Standards	$24.99
00673233	John Coltrane Solos	$27.99
00672328	Paul Desmond Collection	$19.99
00672530	Kenny Garrett Collection	$22.99

00699375	Stan Getz	$19.99
00672377	Stan Getz – Bossa Novas	$22.99
00672375	Stan Getz – Standards	$19.99
00673254	Great Tenor Sax Solos	$22.99
00672523	Coleman Hawkins Collection	$22.99
00672330	Best of Joe Henderson	$24.99
00673239	Best of Kenny G	$22.99
00673229	Kenny G – Breathless	$19.99
00672462	Kenny G – Classics in the Key of G	$22.99
00672485	Kenny G – Faith: A Holiday Album	$17.99
00672373	Kenny G – The Moment	$19.99
00672498	Jackie McLean Collection	$19.95
00672372	James Moody Collection – Sax and Flute	$19.95
00672416	Frank Morgan Collection	$19.95
00672539	Gerry Mulligan Collection	$22.99
00672561	Best of Sonny Rollins	$19.95
00102751	Sonny Rollins, Art Blakey & Kenny Drew with the Modern Jazz Quartet	$17.95
00675000	David Sanborn Collection	$19.99
00672528	The Bud Shank Collection	$19.95
00672491	The New Best of Wayne Shorter	$24.99
00672550	The Sonny Stitt Collection	$19.95
00672524	Lester Young Collection	$19.99

TROMBONE

00672332	J.J. Johnson Collection	$22.99
00672489	Steve Turré Collection	$19.99

TRUMPET

00672557	Herb Alpert Collection	$19.99
00672480	Louis Armstrong Collection	$19.99
00672481	Louis Armstrong Plays Standards	$19.99
00672435	Chet Baker Collection	$22.99
00672556	Best of Chris Botti	$19.99
00672448	Miles Davis – Originals, Vol. 1	$19.99
00672451	Miles Davis – Originals, Vol. 2	$19.95
00672449	Miles Davis – Standards, Vol. 2	$19.95
00672479	Dizzy Gillespie Collection	$19.95
00673214	Freddie Hubbard	$19.99
00672506	Chuck Mangione Collection	$19.99
00672525	Arturo Sandoval – Trumpet Evolution	$19.99

0621

Prices, content, and availability subject to change without notice.

The Best-Selling Jazz Book of All Time Is Now Legal!

The Real Books are the most popular jazz books of all time. Since the 1970s, musicians have trusted these volumes to get them through every gig, night after night. The problem is that the books were illegally produced and distributed, without any regard to copyright law, or royalties paid to the composers who created these musical masterpieces.

Hal Leonard is very proud to present the first legitimate and legal editions of these books ever produced. You won't even notice the difference, other than all the notorious errors being fixed: the covers and typeface look the same, the song lists are nearly identical, and the price for our edition is even cheaper than the originals!

Every conscientious musician will appreciate that these books are now produced accurately and ethically, benefitting the songwriters that we owe for some of the greatest tunes of all time!

VOLUME 1
00240221	C Edition	$39.99
00240224	B♭ Edition	$39.99
00240225	E♭ Edition	$39.99
00240226	Bass Clef Edition	$39.99
00286389	F Edition	$39.99
00240292	C Edition 6 x 9	$35.00
00240339	B♭ Edition 6 x 9	$35.00
00147792	Bass Clef Edition 6 x 9	$35.00
00451087	C Edition on CD-ROM	$29.99
00200984	Online Backing Tracks: Selections	$45.00
00110604	Book/USB Flash Drive Backing Tracks Pack	$79.99
00110599	USB Flash Drive Only	$50.00

VOLUME 2
00240222	C Edition	$39.99
00240227	B♭ Edition	$39.99
00240228	E♭ Edition	$39.99
00240229	Bass Clef Edition	$39.99
00240293	C Edition 6 x 9	$35.00
00125900	B♭ Edition 6 x 9	$35.00
00451088	C Edition on CD-ROM	$30.99
00125900	The Real Book – Mini Edition	$35.00
00204126	Backing Tracks on USB Flash Drive	$50.00
00204131	C Edition – USB Flash Drive Pack	$79.99

VOLUME 3
00240233	C Edition	$39.99
00240284	B♭ Edition	$39.99
00240285	E♭ Edition	$39.99
00240286	Bass Clef Edition	$39.99
00240338	C Edition 6 x 9	$35.00
00451089	C Edition on CD-ROM	$29.99

VOLUME 4
00240296	C Edition	$39.99
00103348	B♭ Edition	$39.99
00103349	E♭ Edition	$39.99
00103350	Bass Clef Edition	$39.99

VOLUME 5
00240349	C Edition	$39.99
00175278	B♭ Edition	$39.99
00175279	E♭ Edition	$39.99

VOLUME 6
00240534	C Edition	$39.99
00223637	E♭ Edition	$39.99

Also available:
00154230	The Real Bebop Book	$34.99
00240264	The Real Blues Book	$34.99
00310910	The Real Bluegrass Book	$35.00
00240223	The Real Broadway Book	$35.00
00240440	The Trane Book	$22.99
00125426	The Real Country Book	$39.99
00269721	The Real Miles Davis Book C Edition	$24.99
00269723	The Real Miles Davis Book B♭ Edition	$24.99
00240355	The Real Dixieland Book C Edition	$32.50
00294853	The Real Dixieland Book E♭ Edition	$35.00
00122335	The Real Dixieland Book B♭ Edition	$35.00
00240235	The Duke Ellington Real Book	$22.99
00240268	The Real Jazz Solos Book	$30.00
00240348	The Real Latin Book C Edition	$37.50
00127107	The Real Latin Book B♭ Edition	$35.00
00120809	The Pat Metheny Real Book C Edition	$27.50
00252119	The Pat Metheny Real Book B♭ Edition	$24.99
00240358	The Charlie Parker Real Book C Edition	$19.99
00275997	The Charlie Parker Real Book E♭ Edition	$19.99
00118324	The Real Pop Book – Vol. 1	$35.00
00240331	The Bud Powell Real Book	$19.99
00240437	The Real R&B Book C Edition	$39.99
00276590	The Real R&B Book B♭ Edition	$39.99
00240313	The Real Rock Book	$35.00
00240323	The Real Rock Book – Vol. 2	$35.00
00240359	The Real Tab Book	$32.50
00240317	The Real Worship Book	$29.99

THE REAL CHRISTMAS BOOK
00240306	C Edition	$32.50
00240345	B♭ Edition	$32.50
00240346	E♭ Edition	$35.00
00240347	Bass Clef Edition	$32.50
00240431	A-G CD Backing Tracks	$24.99
00240432	H-M CD Backing Tracks	$24.99
00240433	N-Y CD Backing Tracks	$24.99

THE REAL VOCAL BOOK
00240230	Volume 1 High Voice	$35.00
00240307	Volume 1 Low Voice	$35.00
00240231	Volume 2 High Voice	$35.00
00240308	Volume 2 Low Voice	$35.00
00240391	Volume 3 High Voice	$35.00
00240392	Volume 3 Low Voice	$35.00
00118318	Volume 4 High Voice	$35.00
00118319	Volume 4 Low Voice	$35.00

Complete song lists online at www.halleonard.com

Prices, content, and availability subject to change without notice.

0719
318